A Good Place

*Walking with Hope through the Transitions
of Life and Ministry*

Garris Elkins

Prophetic Horizons
Jacksonville, Oregon
United States

A Good Place: Walking with Hope through the Transitions of Life and Ministry.

Prophetic Horizons
PO Box 509
Jacksonville, OR 97530 USA
info@prophetichorizons.com
www.garriselkins.com

ISBN-13: 978-0615947570
ISBN-10: 0615947573

Cover design and image, "A Good Place," by Anna Elkins

Printed in the United States of America.

Dedication

I dedicate this book to those of you who are in the midst of a life transition. This will be a journey of the heart. Everyone eventually arrives at the end of a transition, but not everyone finishes well. The purpose of these pages is to help you end your transition with your heart still tender toward God and toward those with whom you have traveled.

Contents

"For I know the plans I have for you," says the Lord. "They are plans for good and not for disaster, to give you a future and a hope."
—Jeremiah 29:11

Introduction

This book began as a compilation of single thoughts on life transitions that developed into the expanded format you now hold in your hands. Over the last thirty-plus years, I have made several major life transitions and helped others do the same.

I learned something from each transition. I learned what I did right—though so much of it could have been done better—and I learned where I had failed. The basic lesson in each of these transitions has remained the same—it just took on new names and occurred in different places. The lesson I repeatedly discovered: God is faithful.

We usually don't do transitions well. We can always do them much better. Our plans for transition are generally not bad, but the condition of our hearts can derail the best of plans. It is my hope that the insights I share in this book might become part of your contemplative process as you enter a life transition or as you engage a process of a transition already in motion. As you read, allow God access to your heart and motives, for it is in these two areas that the greatest battles are fought.

God is good, and all he does is good. Your transition can deposit you in a good place if you accept God's invitation to walk with him through the changing seasons of life.

One day you will make your final life transition. On that day, you will stand in the presence of the one who promised never to leave you or forsake you, no matter how challenging your life has been.

This book is about trusting in a good God in the midst of transitions and trusting his plan to deliver you into a good place.

Suggestions for the Reader

There are many good resources already published on how to create a plan and structure for transition. This book is not about a plan or structure or the details of a transition. *A Good Place* is a book about the condition of our hearts toward God and people as we walk out our journeys to a new place.

I constructed this book similar to a devotional. Each insight is broken down into three parts: a transitional thought, a few paragraphs developing a deeper understanding of that thought, and then a suggested prayer.

Open and honest conversations create an honoring environment in any transition, and I hope you can use some of these thoughts to prepare yourself and your team for the best possible transition.

Though I wrote this book from the perspective of a pastor in a local church, the principles apply to any life transition.

I bless you with ears to hear and eyes to see what the Spirit is saying as you move through the transitions of your life. Hope is always available to you in this walk of faith. That hope is sourced in the promise that he who began this good work in you will be faithful to bring it to completion.

1

The Way Forward

Looking into the future without faith spawns fear. Faith looks into an unexplored future and declares that God is good and that he will be faithful to reveal the way forward.

You are about to enter a journey called *transition*. Dictionaries define this with words like passage, change, and development. Transition is a word that tells us life will not be the same once we enter the process.

Each transition will change us. We change because what is coming requires that our emotional and spiritual shape adjust to the new portal through which we will move. Change is not always an enjoyable experience. Living things change their shape as they grow and develop. Dying things stop changing and remain static in death.

As you begin your transition, ask God for more faith. Your faith comes from God as a gift. When you receive your gift of faith, you will be asked to exercise that gift.

Your faith cannot be placed in the success of the transition or how well you will respond in the process.

Your faith must be placed in God alone. You can entrust your life and this transition to him. He will deliver you into a good future where he already resides. He is there in this moment, extending an invitation for you to take your first step.

Prayer

Father, give me the faith to trust you more than I trust this transition plan I have created. I declare your goodness with each step. Open my eyes to see *you* as the way forward. I entrust myself to you as I begin this journey into something new.

2

A Guiding Word

All healthy transitions move forward with a word from God. Don't move forward until you have that guiding word. It will dig you out of the ruts that are present in each journey.

The Word of God, both written and spoken, has guided your life for years. Why would a word from God not be available to guide you through this transition?

Each transition contains a word from God that will reveal the way forward. Abram had a word. Moses had a word. Joshua had a word. You will also have a word. This word is not something you create. This is *his* word: a word he invites you to engage and live out.

God is faithful to provide a word if you will simply ask him. He has a place he wants to deliver you into: a good place. The word that will lead you is also good because God is good. Goodness is your destination and goodness will be your pathway.

You will experience seasons of sameness where ruts

of familiarity will develop in your life. The word God gives you in this transition will work like a pry bar, leveraging you out of those ruts into the new future he has planned.

Prayer

Father, I open up my heart to receive a word from you about my life and this future transition. I have some ideas, but I want revelation from you. You are the revealer of the way forward. You desire to direct my steps, making me sure-footed and delivering me safely to my destination. It will be your revelation upon which I will rest my head in the doubting night. I will take that word and work with you and faithful friends to build a way forward.

3

Grasping

Without a transition plan, you will be found grasping the doorframe of your current life assignment, afraid to let go and move into the new season God has for you.

Fear can cause us to freeze and become immobile. When faced with a transition, we can sometimes find ourselves holding on to our current assignment in fear of what might not come.

This kind of fear can paralyze us. Instead of believing for more, we settle for less. We grasp onto only what we know, not what we have been asked to believe. Our fear becomes a limiting testimony of how we see God.

In these situations, we stand in the doorway of something new without ever actually stepping across the threshold. God already has your new place prepared. He is simply asking you to let go and trust him. When you let go, God is free to lead you toward your new and unexplored future.

Prayer

Father, I am living in fear of my future. I am afraid of what I cannot yet see. Heal this brokenness in my heart. I want to be willing to trust you enough to let go and believe you have my best interests in mind. You have good intentions for me and those I love. I will step out of this doorframe of fear and cross this new threshold believing that your mercy and forgiveness will greet me on the other side.

4

Too Long

You can stay too long.

I remember talking to a pastor who said he had stayed too long in his current assignment. I had never heard someone say that before. He said he wished he would have departed two years earlier because all the pain and sorrow he experienced in those last two years might not have taken place.

We can stay too long. When we stay too long, things begin to dry up. Life becomes brittle and protective. When we become brittle, our brittleness can lead to fractured responses to those around us.

Staying too long can be an indicator we are trying to squeeze all the life we can out of this present assignment in fear that our future will not be filled with promise. When we stay too long, we become like a driver who depresses the clutch pedal of an automobile but never releases it to engage the next gear. Eventually, our life will coast to a standstill.

Prayer

Father, help me know your timing. I know each season has a beginning and an end. Reveal these to me. I receive from you the courage to let go and begin walking into my future, trusting you with each step.

5
Too Soon

You can leave too soon.

A friend once said to me: "I am not sure if this is the Lord—it might just be the pizza I ate late last night." My friend's disclaimer revealed something to me; we can ascribe things to God that may not be his.

We can get excited at the prospect of something new. New experiences and new seasons appear the most exciting when we want to leave our current assignment.

We all have the ability to make pizza sound like God. Leaving too soon has always been an indicator to me that I wanted to run away instead of engaging the very things in the present situation that would ensure a healthy transition in the future.

When we get restless, we end up resting less. In this place of restlessness, we think that forward motion will be what brings us the answer to our unease. It never does. We just export our unresolved issues into the future where they are born once again in a new place.

Prayer

Father, I admit I am restless. I want to see something happen. I want to ignite a fire, but I know if I ignite the fire, it will be the wrong kind of fire: it will be a strange fire. It will consume people and situations in a wrong way. In Jesus' name, I invite your peace to come. I want to be consumed by your peace in this moment. Help me to not run ahead of you like an impatient child.

6

Plan Now

A good time to plan for your future transition is now.

Some people are uncomfortable making plans. Others make too many and never carry them out. Those who make no plans generally go nowhere. Those who make too many plans can end up in neurotic places.

Some people wait until the last minute to begin planning. This kind of planning becomes noisy, hurried, and visually energetic when all the parts begin to collide with each other, demanding that someone make a decision.

The plan for your eventual transition needs to start the day you step into any new assignment. This is not about building a ten-year plan. This is about how you choose to lead with release and succession in mind. Your transition may be twenty years in the future, but start planning now. An early planning mindset releases peace into the process.

Prayer

Father, I offer you a clean sheet of paper on which I can begin to write out the plans you have for me. I have some thoughts, but I really need a word from you. Right now, I hold a pen over this blank page. I am listening. Help me write my future with the ink of hope and trust.

7

Legacy

Resist the urge to craft your own legacy in your departure. This is something we cannot write for ourselves honestly or accurately.

The longer I am alive, the more I have come to realize that writing a personal legacy can end up being a dishonest or, at best, a very one-sided image of a life. Legacies are something other people write for us.

In each transition I walked through, I found myself wanting to be remembered in a certain way. *Faithful, strong,* and *prophetic* are words I would have written about myself. The reality is that many times I was faithless, weak, and shortsighted.

The best legacy writers portray the contrast between our strength and weakness. In God's Kingdom, our strengths must be yielded in order to produce good fruit. God promises to manifest his presence and power in our places of weakness. We want those who write our legacy to be people who write honestly about our lives, hopefully with the pen of honor.

Prayer

Father, I have some puffed up ideas about my life. I also have some realistic ideas about the life I have lived. I invite and receive your help to live in honesty, never demanding that others see me as I would wish but rather in the light of your grace. Fill me with your profound love to such a degree that my legacy leaves a trail of glory pointing to you.

8

Pastor Emeritus

"Pastor Emeritus" can be a title that tells others: "I am having trouble letting go."

I have some friends who use the term, "Pastor Emeritus," to describe the new season of life they entered after transitioning out of their primary leadership role in the church. Their use of that term is personal for them.

Each of us will find ourselves placed in a long line of faithful men and women who have served or will serve throughout the history of the churches we pastor. Each of us made a unique contribution.

If a church remains healthy, it will survive each of us. Some of the contributions we made were good, and some were not so good.

I don't want to leave behind the impression that my season at the helm was the pinnacle in our church's history. I don't want my remembrance to be a rock of success in the middle of the road that every leader who follows me will have to step over in order to move forward.

Every previous and future pastor of our church will be emeritus in his or her own unique way.

Prayer

Father, I know I am a special creation. But no matter how special I am, I will never be your favorite. Your word says you have no favorites. Thank you for reminding me that I am special in my own unique way, but I am not special to the point that my life and contribution is greater than those who have gone before me or those who will come after me. I am grateful for your help in seeing my position within the entire Church body.

9

An Unseen Place

God is waiting for you in a place you cannot
yet see and you think might not even exist.

God is always waiting for us in our future—in a place
of promise we have not yet discovered. God does not ask
us to walk forward into a future where he does not already
reside. That fact comforts us because it would be difficult
to step forward in faith if we thought we would arrive
alone in a place not occupied by God.

Understanding that God will be there to meet us
builds our faith. Like Moses standing before the Red Sea
or the spies returning from the unconquered Promise
Land, we are to believe God has a way across and into the
new place we do not yet see. His invitation to come into
an undiscovered future is always extended from that future
place.

We have to be careful not to believe this future place
exists only if we create it. In this kind of thinking, we
become the ones responsible to create our future. We can
forget the words of God to Jeremiah about his plans for

good and a future filled with hope. This was God's plan for Jeremiah. God was in that future place telling Jeremiah what it looked like.

When we fail to see God in our future we can, in essence, become a god responsible for our own good. The passages into our future are not successfully negotiated by human might or intellect. These transitions are made with the help of God who is already there in our future calling us forward.

Prayer

Jesus, help me see with the eyes of the Spirit. Open my eyes and unplug my ears to be receptive to your direction. I choose to believe you are there, in my future, calling me forward into your goodness and peace.

10

Over-Corrected

Transitions are like cars: if over-corrected, they get out of control and crash.

When we over-control our lives, we lose a sense of wonder and mystery. Some people have so over-planned and controlled every aspect of their lives that they have taken on the sole responsibility for the realization of their future destination. To the natural mind, this makes sense. In the spirit, it becomes tragic.

God is creative. His creativity did not end when he created the world and said, "It is good." He is still creating. He is creating new futures. As he creates a new future for you, he is also inviting you into the creative process where new and unexpected things take place. Some of these creative moments can be quite surprising—full of wonder and mystery. These are the surprises that take place when we are in relationship with the Living God.

The longer we live, the more we realize the importance of holding this life loosely—and the plans we make even more loosely. When we tightly grip our spiritual steering wheel and try to force a turn to the left or right, we can end up over-controlling our transition and actually cause the process to lose traction and spin out.

Prayer

Lord, help me relax and enjoy the ride with you. We have a destination in mind, but I want to be free enough to hear you say to me, "Take that left," and wander with you down a spiritual country road to see something new that was not part of my travel plan. I trust your navigation.

11

Unsolicited Criticism

When unsolicited criticism comes, don't dismiss it in total. Ask this question: "Jesus, is there anything in what was said that I need to hear?"

At some point in each transition, you will receive unsolicited criticism and suggestions. Everybody has an opinion. Choose to be large enough in your spirit to be willing to review each of these, even those that appear absurd. Embedded somewhere in such suggestions may be the very thing God wants you to hear. Ask the Lord: "Is there anything in that comment you want me to hear?"

Sometimes, a critical piece of information we might need in order to make a healthy transition can be packaged in the most unlikely form. God may place a piece of information inside the comment of your critic to test the condition of your heart. Having the right information is not enough. We need a right heart attitude in which to house the wisdom we receive.

Prayer

Lord, I want to have a large heart attitude—large enough to not be offended by the package you use to deliver truth to me. Forgive me for the snap judgments I have made about people who rub me the wrong way. I renounce those judgments and any authority they released contrary to your will. I give you permission to speak to me in any way you choose.

12

Retrieving the Promises

Retrieve the promises you have from God and speak them into this transition.

Every season in your life and every transition you walk through will have a promise assigned to it. The children of Israel entered the Promise Land with a promise. The Early Church did not leave Jerusalem until the promised Spirit came. You will not move successfully through this transition without a promise. Everything given to us is the result of a promise God has made.

Promises are powerful because, when spoken, they become a gathering point to assemble the supernatural resources of God that make the promise become a reality. It is important for you to actually speak out the promises of God. Spoken promises interrupt the environment of the status quo and call forth something new. A spoken promise can become the turning point in a transition.

If you feel like you have no promise, you have not been listening close enough to what God is saying. Ask God to share again with you the promises he has made over your life. As you wait, you will hear things that may sound presumptive or border on the absurd. Trust God that he has good and wonderful promises ready to release into your life.

Prayer

Father, I know you make promises to your children. I am your child, and you want me to live with the expectancy that a life of promise brings. I am expectant. You have promised me that I will not be diminished in the waiting. In fact, I am growing larger within your promise. I call to remembrance the words you have spoken over me. Open my eyes and ears to perceive your truth. I will declare your promises and choose to believe that as I speak them over my life you are at work making them a reality.

13

Elements

We all have a tendency to see each life transition as an isolated event, but transitions are one of many elements that make up the larger journey of life.

Life is a collection of journeys, not just a single trip. Each journey has a measure of faith assigned to it that we are to ask God to release. Without this measure of faith, we will process the journey only with natural sight and without assurance for those parts of the transition we cannot yet see.

We have the tendency to over-focus on what is immediate and visible. Our myopic vision actually blurs our ability to see the lessons learned from past experiences. God uses those lessons to help us plan in the present a successful transition into the future.

You may need to walk away—far enough away from what is before you so that you can gain a new perspective and see your life from a panoramic point of view. Has God ever failed you? Has he ever not provided a way for you in the past? It is time to see how faithful God has been in the past so that you don't have fear about what is developing in your future.

Prayer

Today, I want to find the journey within the journey. Lord, help me see where your hands are waiting to take hold of my life. Your hands are my steppingstones—stones along the path of the larger journey of my life. You are forever faithful. You are my journey.

14

The Open Door

A new opportunity does not always lead us to God's preferred future for our lives. The wise wait and ask God if he has opened the door before them.

We like having options. Our culture has taught us to value choice, and we are provided with a multitude of choices. If we aren't careful, we can choose a wrong doorway and enter into something God never intended for us to experience. How can we test a doorway to know if it has been opened by God? The answer is found in the test of peace.

Over the years, this test of peace has never failed me. The test lines up all the available options and asks a simple question: which of these opportunities carries the peace of God?

This peace is not the absence of external conflict. This is a peace that resides in our hearts away from the influence of our circumstances. This peace is far beyond our ability to understand how and why we possess it.

In your transition, you will need to discover the evidence of this peace before you start making changes about the direction of your life. Peace will lead you to the Prince of Peace, and his peace will protect you. Peace is the doorway through which God will lead you into your future.

Prayer

Jesus, give me the ability to perceive your peace amidst the whirlwind of life. I am trying to figure out each and every aspect of this transition, and it is robbing me of my peace. You are the Prince of Peace, and I accept your invitation to exchange my restlessness for your peace. I am asking for your wisdom in this transition so that all the decisions I make will be the product of your peace.

15

Make a Way

God used your spiritual gifts to make a way for you into your current assignment, and he will use them to make a way into your next assignment.

Somewhere along the way, God deposited supernatural gifts in your life that he will use to accomplish his purpose and calling for your life. These gifts were part of what God has used to bring you to this place.

These supernatural gifts are often deposited in us through the laying on of hands. We read about this impartation in the second letter Paul wrote to Timothy. Timothy had become so busy with life and ministry that he allowed the intensity of those gifts to diminish from a flame to a smoldering ember. Both of Paul's letters to Timothy contain warnings about the dimming condition of his gifts. Paul told Timothy to fan the embers into a flame once again.

The longer we do life and ministry, the easier it becomes for us to operate in our own strength. We develop skill sets. We get good at what we do. Subtly, we can begin to exchange the power of God for human ability. This becomes especially dangerous when we are transitioning into a new season and crossing into unexplored territory.

God placed gifts in your life to do what he has called you to do; you cannot fulfill your calling without exercising them. Like Paul instructed Timothy, you need to stir up your gifts so they are white-hot with potential to accomplish the spiritual passage that lies before you.

Prayer

Father, I place my trust in you, the giver of gifts. Forgive me for relying on my developed skills and my natural abilities. Today, I reach inside my life by faith and stir up the supernatural deposit you have placed there. You have planned my transition with these gifts in mind. I embrace the role they will play in this process. I speak to my heart and mind to be bold and obedient to use these gifts. I declare the embers to become flames once again, and I desire to live with the expectancy that you have new gifts for a new place.

16

Judgment Calls

Go back and repent of the judgment calls you made on the leaders who went before you in your current assignment. This is for the sake and safety of your transition and your future.

Unrighteous judgments will end conversations and, eventually, relationships. When we discern sin in people, we can easily become judgmental and distance ourselves from those we judge.

We create walls. God tears down walls.

God righteously judged our sin, did away with it, and then invited us to come to him and receive freedom.

Freedom and judgment do not dwell together in harmony. When we judge others in a wrong way, we can actually become like the judgments we made. Our judgments make us blind to our own sin. Jesus asked us to judge the fruit of a life as an act of discernment. This discernment gives us the ability to see with the eyes of the Spirit. We discern things to become part of the solution.

He never asks us to judge a person in order to throw them away.

Those who went before us made mistakes. We have also made mistakes during our assignment. We must be merciful as we examine the lives of those who went before us. Someday, someone will examine our lives, and we will want them to extend mercy to us.

Prayer

Lord, forgive me for judging [fill in a name]. Forgive me for not believing the best about them. In your name, Jesus, I confess and renounce that judgment. I renounce any authority given to the enemy, and I take that authority back. Your mercy will always triumph over judgment. I receive your mercy, and I extend your mercy to anyone I will follow in this assignment.

17

Exposure

Every transition will reveal your insecurities. One of the gifts of transition is exposure. God sheds light on us so he can heal us and prepare us for what is coming.

Transitions are like sandpaper—they sand away our sense of security and reveal where we have placed our trust. The deeper we walk into a life change, the harder the transitional sandpaper works. We begin to see our true self, hidden beneath schedules, success, or sin.

God loves us so much. He wants the next phase of our lives to be healthier than the one we are now living. God will dig deeper to reveal the layers of personal brokenness we have used as deflective shields against the healing work of his Spirit.

The sanding away of these personal illusions is part of the preparation for what is to come. Don't resist it. Offer God all of you so that in the end he will have shaped you more and more into the image of his Son.

Prayer

Father, this transition feels like I'm being scoured with gritty sandpaper. Some of my protective layers are being compromised. I am seeing things I thought we had dealt with years before. Even though it is uncomfortable, I choose to yield to you and face this discomfort, allowing you to shape my life to fit the future you have prepared for me.

18

Emerging Leaders

Emerging leaders need room. The transitioning leader should make a place for a new gift to function in relationship without unnecessary restriction.

None of us make good decisions when we feel crowded. When people crowd us out of a process or press in over our shoulder, they don't allow us the freedom to make our own decisions.

When your successor is invited to the process of transition, give them space—especially with a younger leader. You have a proven track record. They are trying to build one. They will need you to grant them permission to lead. They should not have to fight you or the institutional system to gain that permission.

At this stage, time becomes one of the most important ingredients in a transition. Giving a transition enough time to develop allows the participants the space they need to struggle through their personal adjustments. Remember, you are a spiritual parent, not a competitor.

Give those who follow you the room they need to lead, even before you officially pass them the baton.

Prayer

Father, heal my insecurities. I confess the pride of position. I confess the need I have to be seen as the one on top of the heap—as the most visible leader. Forgive me for seeking prominence and needing personal promotion at the expense of releasing the next generation of leadership. I ask for your help to walk in authority *and* humility.

19

Please Don't Leave Me

The voices that cry the loudest, "Please don't leave!" come from the ones who may need you to leave the most.

People like security. Your current position and influence as a leader—assuming you are healthy in soul and spirit—is a security to some people. You have fed people spiritually. You have celebrated and mourned with them through many life events. It is healthy and honoring that people would love you.

But there comes a time for you to move into a new season. Your moving on will create change, and change will make some people uncomfortable. Your transition will disrupt their sense of stability and security. Change has a rippling effect that will touch everyone influenced by your leadership.

Early in your transition process, begin to speak to people about where their true stability comes from: God. Not pastors, bosses, parental figures, or anyone in authority. God is their Rock. Introduce people to their new future by helping them put their trust in God as they let go of what is known and secure.

Prayer

Jesus, I want to be wanted. Thank you for creating in us the need for community. I don't want this need to be linked to one person but to the larger work of your Spirit in our midst. I stand with these people I have served, declaring your truth over all of us. Your ways are higher than our ways. Your thoughts are higher than our thoughts. We can trust in your promise to never leave us or forsake us, no matter what kind of change we experience.

20

Up to Speed

Once you realize a change is needed, you are usually a bit late. But don't worry if you think you have missed an opportunity. God knows how to accelerate things to bring your transition up to speed and in line with his plan.

There are times in each transition when we feel like we may have missed God's timing. We can feel like our best opportunity has passed us by. In these moments, we need to trust God to make things right.

God loves us. He wants us to understand his heart. He doesn't want us to miss any opportunity he has created. He will do anything within his power to align our lives once again with his purpose.

God knows how to accelerate a missed opportunity to make it a present possession. Don't linger in a place of worry, fretting over what you might have missed. Give God those missed opportunities so they will not become regrets that can immobilize your life and open the door to self-pity. Let God handle the missed opportunities.

Prayer

Jesus, I receive your mercy for the sorrow and regret I am experiencing over this missed opportunity. I know what I missed has value and was intended to accompany me in this present journey. Instead of regretting, I trust that you will return to me what needs to be in my possession as I continue to move forward.

21

The Greatest Battle

In a life transition, one of the greatest battles you will face is to believe the best.

When the reality of what we know and are comfortable with starts to change, we can easily become insecure because the things we once controlled are no longer within our control. And when we're not in control, we can begin to believe the worst.

Fear speaks the loudest when we feel our destiny is outside our control. We can begin listening to lies. If we allow these lies to remain unchallenged, we make room for a negative mental dialogue to develop that talks us into believing that we have a hopeless future.

We fight the worst by choosing to believe the best about God and people. God is the supplier of the best. He is the one who is bringing a good future your way. Trust makes a way for hope, and hope is the hinge that your transition will swing upon. As you walk through this doorway, you will be imprinted with heaven, and you will carry that imprint into your next assignment.

Prayer

Father, help me believe the best. I know this is my choice. I am the one charged with believing. Today, I choose to see the developing doorway before me as a place of joy hinged with hope—a place where you have the best planned for me.

22

A Lesson Revisited

The lessons you learned in past transitions
will help guide you in your future transition.
Revisit those lessons and learn them again.

Just like professional athletes revisit the basics of their sport with their coach, so the followers of Christ revisit the early truths God deposited in them.

Your current understanding of life has been constructed from those foundational truths, so if you neglected or discarded them, revisiting them will help you reconnect and finish well.

Early truths are not inferior truths. Basic training for soldiers establishes cohesiveness in the military unit. Those basic disciplines help keep casualties to a minimum and provide a commander with soldiers who have learned to obey his commands.

Any time we have success, we are susceptible to the illusion that our success birthed itself. Success does not birth success. Love and faithfulness in all areas of life is what births the fruit of success. This kind of success—

sourced in God's Kingdom—is not always large and visible in a natural sense. It is a success that can be traced back to those early lessons we learned through love, faith, and obedience.

Prayer

Jesus, bring to my remembrance the early seasons when you first spoke to me. As I began in the Spirit, help me end in the Spirit—not in my own strength. Imprint in me the value of those early truths, and help me rediscover the profound impact they will have in shaping my future.

23

Proving Our Worth

Bondage is anything we do to prove our worth.

We are and are becoming who we already are. We have been placed in Jesus at the right hand of the Father in eternity. In that place, we are full and complete in Christ. We live this current life from the reality of that present eternal position. This life will eventually be no more. Our position in Christ will remain unchanged throughout all eternity.

We have gained all the worth we will ever possess. Our worth was given to us the day we received the gift of forgiveness through Jesus Christ. In Him we were made fully worthy.

Because we have already been placed in the final destination of our life journey, we never have to struggle to gain worth. Trying to prove our worth in any way is bondage. Bondage is a self-inflicted wound.

We pick up bondage whenever we try to prove our worth to God by doing anything to validate that worth. If at any point in this transition you feel unworthy, stop. Stop and deal with that lie before you do anything else. God wants you to experience life and freedom. That is why he set you free before the journey began.

Prayer

Jesus, give me the eyes to see my life from your perspective—from heaven's perspective. Let me see my life as I am, in this moment, in you and seated at the Father's right hand. I admit that any attempt I have made to create personal worth is a sin, and I confess it as such. Those attempts came because I did not fully understand the price you paid for me. In you I am worthy.

24

An Invitation

Invite people to your transition narrative early in the process. This creates a partnership and lessens the possibility of a fearful response.

We think we protect a transition by keeping it quiet until we are deep within its process. Our motivation can be from fear that people will object to the plan. We think that if we hold off talking about the process we can get it moving at a certain speed, and the momentum created will make us safe from derailment.

What can actually take place is a fear-based response. People don't like to be taken by surprise. People also don't like being left with the impression that they are not intelligent enough to process the transition with you. Hopefully, we don't think we are smart enough to know everything about a planned transition and assume we can run it alone.

A timely dialogue invites people to step into the process with you and explore together the developing narrative of your transition. You have allies yet to be discovered whom God has planted along the way. These people simply need your invitation. Disclosure and transparency form the cardstock upon which that invitation is printed.

Prayer

Spirit of God, help me discover the fear-based elements I have injected into this plan. Uncover those parts of the plan that can create fear in people. Write a narrative for me to speak that extends an invitation early in this process and will help people feel like family and friends, not just observers.

25

Parking Regrets

Park your regrets in the mercy of God.

Regret keeps us looking over our shoulder. Unresolved regrets also keep us anchored in the past. God gave us the ability to move forward beyond our regrets into the hope-filled future he has planned.

Our regrets are an indicator of how we see God. If we missed an opportunity and live in regret, our regret tells us that we have chosen to believe a lie. This lie tells us that God gives us only one opportunity for each circumstance of life. God's mercies are new every morning. The door we should have walked through may never open again, but with God, there will always be another new door of opportunity.

When we live in regret over time, that regret will become clothed in ungodly sorrow, and that kind of sorrow leads to death. The garment of sorrow insulates our regret so that after a while, we begin to think the problem is sorrow. This makes it more challenging to get to the root causes of our regret because our sorrow is saying, "I don't deserve a second chance" or "I don't feel loved."

Prayer

Father, you know each place where I have missed the mark. In these places, I am feeling regret. I ask you to show me the depth of your mercy—the place where you consume sin and the regret of my sin. Forgive me for trying to carry the weight of these regrets. Today, I pick up these regrets, place them in your hands, and call forth your mercy to overwhelm me.

26

Obligation and Discernment

Learn the difference between obligation and discernment. Obligation can have you tied to things you need to let go of in order to make this transition. Discernment will invite you to see the new thing God has planned and will give you permission to let go of the past and embrace the future.

Obligation can become a tether that holds me to the ideas and routines of life that God wants to change as I consider a new future. Discernment is different. Discernment is a gift that reveals what I have not been able to see and invites me to envision something new.

If we allow the Spirit of God to develop in us the ability to hear his quiet whispers, we will be open to make the course adjustments needed to continue our journey forward. As you begin your transition, there will be many voices speaking to you. Some of these voices will be speaking from an obligation to your past. Learn to hear with the discernment that comes from knowing the voice of God. He wants you to be able to discern his invitation apart from all the obligations of life.

Prayer

Father, I want my passion for you to be what fuels my discernment. I want to know you more than I want to know the way forward. I receive your unfailing love and embrace. You have drawn close to me. I choose to draw close to you and to let go of any obligation to the past. I want to walk forward in freedom with you into this new and unfolding future.

27

Finances

A transition will involve the subject of finances. A transition plan should never be directed or held hostage by finances. Follow the word of the Lord first and foremost, and the financial solution will be revealed in the midst of your obedience.

We all need resources from which we can pay our bills and plan for our future. But if our future is defined and engineered solely by financial need, we will begin to construct a future built around the fear of lack. If we fail to deal with this attitude, we will become demanding, grasping, and self-promoting.

God is already present in your future. He knows exactly what you need and don't need. Some of the things you feel you need in order to make this transition could become a burden later on. Some of the things you don't think you need may become essential for you to live and thrive in your new future.

You may have no idea what this future will look like

nor do you see the full picture of his provision. Trust God to supply all you need, and believe that your provision will be waiting for you when you arrive. This is what true financial freedom looks like.

Prayer

Part of me is afraid I won't have enough financial resources available in my future. Lord, I confess this as a fear that reflects a warped understanding of you and your love for me. I entrust myself to you with every detail of this transition, including my finances. I confess and renounce any fear that would try to rob me of the joy that awaits me in this journey. I declare that you have more than enough to meet my needs.

28

Sacrificial Altars

Sometimes, we make sacrifices on altars that do not exist. We can make a sacrifice in a transition when a blessing was God's actual intent.

Some of us need to be set free from thinking our entire experience with God is a sacrifice. Life does include sacrifice, but Jesus came and made the ultimate sacrifice so we could experience joy—even in our suffering. Jesus was obedient because he saw the joy set before him. This kind of joy is always greater than the pain of sacrifice.

We can look ahead and think we are called to build altars for a continuous life of sacrifice and not see the places of celebration. Each altar we construct for a personal sacrifice should be followed by an expression of joy dedicated to celebrating the victory of that sacrifice. Jesus went forward toward the Cross because of the joy set before him.

Prayer

Lord, I confess that I can see life in a negative way. Life is challenging, but not everything you have planned is a challenge or a sacrifice. As I delight myself in you, help me see the celebration you have planned for each place of sacrifice.

29

At Peace

One of the greatest gifts you can leave behind is to be, as far as it is possible with you, at peace with all people.

"As far as possible" means we walk as far forward in the process of reconciliation as the will of the other person will allow. We can walk up onto the emotional porch of another person's life and ring the doorbell, but they must open the door.

Getting up onto this relational porch requires that we do some very visible things to position ourselves in a place of vulnerability. This will require humility. In each season of spiritual growth, there will be some porch time. Healthy transitions will include this element of vulnerability and risk.

God wants us to be free, and he will hand that freedom to us as a medicine to dispense to others. Some people will crack the door open just enough to see you standing on their porch, and that will be enough to begin the process of reconciliation and restoration.

Prayer

In your name, Lord Jesus, I confess and renounce any offense I have picked up against another person. You loved the entire world, not just a select few. You love us all and stand before the door of our hearts with an invitation to wholeness. Help me to be like you in this season of transition and beyond.

30

A New Vision

A new vision is new, not necessarily better.

New is not better. New is different. We have the tendency to think that our turn at the helm navigated the ship of our ministry into its most unique ports. While that sounds good, it is a limited view of God and the future. Something about God is new each morning, and so are the ports of call he has planned for those who will follow you in this assignment.

Our pride wants to enshrine our season as being the truly unique one in the history of a family, a church, or an organization. We all want to feel that our investment was of value. While we all contribute value, our contribution is still only one ingredient in the larger recipe.

Someone is being positioned to follow you. Honor them by allowing them to step forward without having to wear the garment of your reputation and faithful history. Let those who follow you sew their own garments.

Prayer

Lord, I confess a desire that people know the cost I have paid to get us all to where we are. I admit to the fear that I will be forgotten if I don't enshrine my memory somewhere in this transition. I confess this need as the sin of pride. I will be one in a long line of people who worked in this assignment. I ask you to help me regain a humble perspective of my place in history while also being encouraged and grateful for all you have worked in me and through me.

31

A New Team

New ministry teams will get formed without your input. This is not rebellion. This is life. This is change. Embrace it. Support it.

Up to this point, you have probably made most of the decisions in your organization. You were involved in all of the creative conversations. As strange as this will sound, the closer you come to making your transition, the less you should be involved in creating the new model of ministry.

Give yourself permission to be absent. Your absence will say to the team coming after you: "I trust you." If God felt you needed to continue to be the primary decision-maker, he would not have begun leading you on this new journey.

This transition will be filled with integrity checks. How do you respond when a leadership meeting is scheduled, and you were not invited to attend? You might feel rejected. You weren't. You might feel the urge to step back in and pick up the reins. Don't. Take those feelings of insecurity to God, and let him bring healing so you can move forward and so those who follow you don't have to live under the bondage of someone who can't let go.

Prayer

God, it is hard for me to let go. It is the hardest when I don't feel included. If decisions are made without my input, I feel devalued. Thank you for identifying this area of my life that needs to be healed. I will do whatever I can to help the new team live and work in freedom.

32

The Compass

*Your transition plan is not your compass;
God's voice is.*

You might have the plan for your future all laid out in great detail. Plans are wise. In fact, a mark of a wise person is to have a plan. However, don't forget that a single whisper from God can override your plan at any moment.

God is your compass; your well-developed plan isn't. Some things will take place in this transition that may seem to violate the original plan, but they could be course adjustments made in response to the compass.

In these times, it becomes important to remember the transition plan does not give you life and hope: only God can provide those things.

Today, commit yourself to developing a sensitive ear to the voice of God. His course corrections may lead you a bit off the planned course, but in the end they will guide you to a good place.

Prayer

Lord, I like my plan. I want to follow it. I want to arrive safely at where I am going, and this plan is helping me do that. But help me avoid the danger of not exercising faith in you during this transition. I can see the plan. I cannot "see" your voice. Give me the faith and courage to step aside if I need to follow the direction of your voice.

33

A Right Heart

You can remain in the place of your current assignment only if your heart is right and there is honor in the house.

One of the greatest gifts we give to those who follow us is a healthy attitude and a willing heart. Many people, especially as they grow older, will not physically move away once they make their final life transition. They have made friends, bought homes, and settled into the community. The expectation is that they would remain.

If those who follow us are willing to have us remain, our task is to monitor our attitudes and deal with our insecurities so that our presence is a gift, not a burden. Don't shortchange the plans of God by giving negative attitudes a place to grow.

What a tremendous value you could be to the incoming leadership team if you choose to become one of their greatest supporters. This is where your definition of honor will be tested. Let honor win!

Prayer

Father, I want to be an enjoyable and valued part of this team in the future. I would like my presence to bring joy. Help me steer clear of defensive attitudes. I give you any place in my heart where a toxic attitude remains. Come and heal me. I choose to live in honor with you and those around me.

34

The Cliff

Don't view your transition as a cliff where you will eventually fall off into nothing. There are no cliffs with God; they only exist in our minds where fear has been allowed to rule.

Transitions are times when we move into something new. We have a tendency to see life as a series of endings, but this resurrection life is actually a series of new beginnings.

Perceived cliffs are places where we feel that life as we know it is about to end. These fearful cliffs are created out of the false belief that something bad exists beyond our transition date. If your transition has been painful, it will be too easy to project that pain into your emerging future.

God has no cliff planned for your life. God has placed a staircase ahead of you. He is inviting you to take a step of faith upward toward the good place he has prepared.

Prayer

Lord, help me see my future through the lens of faith and not through the fear of loss. It is too easy to see a cliff of despair when I should see a staircase of hope. Let this become the time in my life when I let go of a fear-based vision and look with faith at your goodness that lies before me.

35

The Detour

Telling God where you will go or not go after your transition is the beginning of a detour you might not return from.

When we begin to demand that God show us what our future and its provision will look like, we begin taking a dangerous detour. This is a road paved with fear. This road is protected by the sentinel of self and closes off the voice of God that says, "Trust me."

These demands on God about our future are sourced in the fear that he will not come through for us. A detour begins when we push trust aside and the responsibility of personal provision and direction falls upon our shoulders. We begin to carry burdens that are not ours to bear.

As the process of your life transition deepens, you will need to focus more intentionally on God's voice. This is a time to lean in and strain your ear to hear his whispers. His voice is your only reliable source of direction.

Prayer

God, I lay down my demand for a preferred future. Though I have an idea of the direction I'd like to go, I honestly have no idea what the destination will look like. Forgive me for trusting myself over you. I invite your peace to guide me along this path. I am collecting the detour signs that have cluttered this journey, and I lay them at your feet.

36

Missed Opportunities

Deal with your sorrow over missed opportunities. Trust God, who is raising up new leaders, to collect those missed opportunities and turn them into victories.

A missed opportunity is never really lost. God will raise someone up to discover what you missed.

The leaders you have developed carry your heart. They know what you were passionate about. Try not to attach a sense of failure to the list of missed opportunities in your life. If you do this, you will stop moving forward and get stuck in regret and sadness.

One of the joys you will experience in the coming years is seeing those who followed you discovering your missed opportunities and turning them into victories for God's Kingdom. This will turn your sorrow of a missed opportunity into the joy of a shared discovery.

Prayer

God, I feel a sadness that I have missed some opportunities. Build expectancy in me that this new generation of leaders will discover what was lost in my generation. Teach me how to celebrate these discoveries without regret.

37

Blessing People

Bless when you feel betrayed. Bless when you are offended. Bless when people try to hijack the transition plan. These blessings will protect your heart from growing hard, and they will keep you responsive to the Spirit.

At any point in the transition, something could go wrong—not necessarily with the plan itself but with the people who are living in the plan with you. Your spiritual survival depends on you extending forgiveness, but that alone is not enough.

Forgiveness will be challenged when you rehash the offense in your mind and feel its pain once again. In these challenges, you will see the face of the offender. You will see the group who has bought into the lie. There is something you can do with these images, and that action has a powerful effect: bless the offender and the offended.

Blessing is a form of spiritual warfare. Each time you bless those you have forgiven, you are enforcing that original act of forgiveness. Blessing has the power to turn an enemy into a friend. It can also turn a curse into a blessing. If you choose to live this way, you will see the supernatural hand of God begin to work in ways you never thought possible.

Prayer

Jesus, you forgave us and restored us to the Father. In that restoration came the blessing of renewed relationship. I receive your grace and strength to give that same gift to those who stand at odds with me. You did this for me, and I want to do the same for others. Today, I choose to forgive, and I choose to bless because I have been forgiven and I have been blessed.

38

Creating New Models

We should not continue to create the model of ministry we will give to those who follow us. Invite them early into the transition process to begin developing the new model they will eventually carry.

It is awkward and uncomfortable to ask emerging leaders to assume that every detail of your ministry will become theirs. When we pass on our model, instead of passing on the freedom to hear God, we can create a generation of imitators instead of creators.

It empowers the one who will replace you when you say, "I give you permission to create a new model of ministry that will fit your gifts." This becomes especially empowering when done before you hand over the reins of your leadership; it gives the new leader time to create and tailor a ministry garment that fits them.

When you allow the new leader to be creative while you are still at the helm, you build mutual trust equity. You also help those who are observing the change in leadership develop a deeper trust in you and the incoming leader. If you both are good with the development of a new ministry model, it will make it easier for the entire church community to find confidence in the transition.

Prayer

Father, I ask for the gift of courage. I need courage to let go before this transition is complete. Help me let go today and allow this new leader the space required to flex his gifts in the security that comes from knowing he is relating to a spiritual father, not a competitor.

39

Behind the Scenes

When you feel the transition is being aborted, don't forget that God is always at work behind the scenes birthing something new.

Birth is a miracle. Getting a baby through the various trimesters of pregnancy is also a miracle. Each stage is critical in the development of a healthy child.

The same is true in a change of leadership. There may be times when something doesn't feel right. You rush to the spiritual emergency room and wait for the doctor. You may find out that you missed an important part of your birthing plan. You feel that without this part, the process could be aborted.

Here is where you get to trust God. None of this has taken him by surprise. Something may have died, but God is always birthing something new. He may even rewrite your entire transition plan to get you and all the participants to full term.

Prayer

Father, it feels like this plan might be aborted. Help me find rest while you reveal the next step to me. I know you are at work behind what is visible. I declare that you are good all the time. I can trust you. I stand in your mercy in this place where things seem to be going wrong. I declare your justice where injustice wants to reign. What the enemy has tried to kill, I call forth into life.

40

Believe

Believe the best.

Every process involves moments when fear wants to take hold, and our imagination begins working at hyperspeed. We imagine scenarios with people and situations that do not exist. Our fear triggers defensive and self-protecting arguments, causing us to do battle on imaginary battlefields.

Choosing to believe the best is a rebuke to the lies that hover over our lives looking for a place to land. When we believe the worst, we provide the enemy with a landing zone for his lies and give him the ability to set up supply lines to increase his presence and effect.

I have tested this and found that when I believed the worst, it rarely happened. I had wasted my time and my peace. Usually, when I believed the best—the good thing God had planned—it became a reality. Believing the best is an act of spiritual warfare.

Prayer

Father, today I choose to believe the best about people and circumstances. I will confront the lies that rise up in the places of my own insecurity and fear. I know that people respond to life out of their own pain and sorrow, and those responses aren't about me. Help me confound those who are acting like they are my enemy by extending forgiveness and mercy to them. Today, I choose to live in the expectation that the best is coming my way.

41

Unraveled Plans

When a life plan begins to unravel, God knows how to reweave all the disconnected parts into something better.

When a well-thought plan begins to unravel, our first response can be to grab all the frayed ends and try to put them back together again. I want to suggest that the unraveling is not always a bad thing. Sometimes God will allow a process to unravel so he can reweave the elements back together into something stronger.

Our transition can become so planned and well executed that at some point we stop exercising faith. We end up going with the flow of the plan and fail to yield our lives in faith each day.

None of us likes things to come undone. It feels uncomfortable and disorganized. God is bigger than these scenarios. Give him your frayed and disconnected ends. Watch him begin to weave the plan back together. When he is done, he will hand the tapestry back to you stronger and more beautiful than it was before the problems arose.

Prayer

Father, some of this process has come undone. Will you take the plan and reweave it? I want to display this restored tapestry so that those who see it know you restored it. Nothing is ever lost, no matter how unraveled it has become, if I allow you to reweave its image.

42

The Rescue

In a transition, you will never find yourself in a situation where God does not have a plan of rescue in place. Trust him.

Ship captains don't start their sea voyages by planning to sink. Neither do we start our transitions by planning to sink. However, there may come a time when you experience a storm, a "perfect storm," when all the elements for disaster come together and threaten the transition.

These are relational storms that have dangerous reefs of distrust, winds of betrayal, and waves of conflict that seem too high for your current level of faith. These storms break your heart. Your future and family face uncertainty. Havoc seems to fill the air, and you have nowhere to run because you are trapped on the open seas of transitional turmoil.

In the stormy moments when you think all is lost, call out to God. He has a plan to help you ride through the storm to a safe harbor.

And sometimes, he will supernaturally calm the storm first and have you move forward across calm waters.

Prayer

I cry out to you, God! I feel like I am going to drown in this storm. I don't know where all this turmoil came from. We started this voyage with a calm weather report, and then everything got stormy. I feel afraid and threatened on these waves. Calm my heart, Lord. You are good all the time, and I can trust you. I will not let fear rob me of this trust.

43

Change

The older we get, the less we want to experience change. Living things are always changing. Without change we get "old" and brittle.

I have noticed senior citizens trying to dress and act like twenty-somethings. It never works. There is something right and confident about being comfortable in our age-specific skin.

We fight against change by trying to live in the past, and in doing so, we miss the powerful assignment God has for us in the present.

One of the most visible indicators that we are a living being is change. God changes us through each season of life. He also changes us in each transition we experience.

Give yourself permission to change in this transition. Expect change. Some things might get changed that you felt would always remain the same. Be open and willing to grow older gracefully, and you will experience something new.

Prayer

Lord, you said to come to you as a child. You said this to young and old alike. Give me the heart of a child in this transition so I can be fully alive and engaged in the new thing you are about to do.

44

Spiritual Parents

If you are a spiritual father or mother, you will find joy in what makes your children joyful.

As parents, we get our greatest joy from seeing joy in the eyes of our children. This is also true for spiritual parents. We get our greatest joy from seeing our spiritual children happy and thriving in God.

If you are older than those who are assuming your leadership role, this understanding of joy becomes especially important. Don't let the transition become a corporate or business plan. Keep it family, and joy will be present in the process.

Each leader is a spiritual parent. You will know you have made a healthy life transition when the joy you have as a spiritual parent is seen most clearly in the eyes of those who follow you.

Prayer

Father, you experience joy when you see your children happy and functioning to the fullest in their gifts and calling. Give me that kind of a parent's heart. I will celebrate with those who follow me. Give them more, and take them farther and higher than I have ever gone. I want them to see joy in me so they will know that I am with them and have their best interests in mind.

45

Night Voices

Nighttime can be the worst time. This is when hell often speaks the loudest and tries to turn your rest into restlessness.

Fatigue in life and ministry does not come from a packed schedule. We can be busy but live in rest. In times of transition, our fatigue comes when our minds are filled with unresolved conflict and fear about the future. We lay in bed and cannot turn off the voices of fear that occupy our mind.

Fatigue takes fear to a dark place. That dark place is where our hope is robbed, and our joy is extinguished. To combat this kind of fatigue, we must resolve to not worry about the future. This is easy to say but challenging to do. We make this resolution in the assurance that God is in our future waiting for us with his love and goodness. His presence in our future is what brings peace to this present moment.

Take your thoughts prisoner. March them to the feet of Jesus and leave them there. This is your place of rest.

Prayer

Lord, I know that I am not at rest. I want to rest, but I find I am struggling to do so. Help me find the peace that only you can give—a peace that is beyond human reasoning. I can entrust myself to you without needing to have all the answers. I give you my restlessness and receive your peace in exchange.

46

A Spiritual Terrorist

Self-pity is a spiritual terrorist who wants to sneak aboard your life. This destructive attitude comes with a bomb strapped to its back. Detonate it in prayer—far away from innocent bystanders.

The problem with self-pity is that it feels so good. Like a drug, it feeds a false reality and the accompanying illusions that justify its existence.

Somewhere in this transition, you may feel slighted. You might even feel betrayed or ignored. In these times, your emotions will be intensified. You will need to walk with wisdom so that your response to people is directed by the Spirit, not by your emotions.

None of what's taking place is personal. It can feel personal, but most often what is happening is simply a manifestation of your insecurity during a time of change.

Your best course of action is to acknowledge self-pity, confess it, and let God heal you. This is best done in private or with a trusted prayer partner before you say something publicly that could wound people who have no idea of what you are struggling with. Deal with your heart. Then, if you do need to approach anyone who hurt you, you will go with a right heart attitude. A right heart attitude makes positive change possible.

Prayer

Father, I have yielded to the destructive force of self-pity. I confess it feels good to argue with these emotions in isolation where I have no one to confront me. Forgive me for buying into the lie of self-pity. I yield to you my "right" to live this way.

47

Your First Response

If you are faced with what appears to be the total collapse of your transition plan, your first and most important response is worship.

When we find ourselves deep into a transition and experience a betrayal or the loss of trust on a personal level, the transition can appear to be falling apart. Few things feel more devastating.

When betrayal occurs, it feels like someone hit us in the stomach as hard as they could and walked away leaving us writhing on the floor in pain. In those moments, it is too easy to react and try to defend yourself or make the other party pay for their betrayal. Resist this urge.

The best course of action is to drop to your knees and begin to worship. Worship God for his faithfulness. Worship God for his goodness. Worship God because he sees the beginning and the end.

The reason we worship in times of tremendous loss is because only worship is able to refocus our lives and free us from revenge, paybacks, and defensive plans. Worship allows us to place our wound in the presence of God where his Spirit is able to bring comfort and healing. Worship gives the outcome to God where it will be free from our manipulative input.

Prayer

Father, this hurts like nothing I have ever experienced. I feel betrayed and lost. You said you would keep me in perfect peace. I receive that promise. In the midst of this confusion, I choose to worship you, I declare you are good, and I acknowledge that you know how to walk me through this field of broken relationships.

48

Directed Steps

We can make our plans, but in the end, it is the Lord who directs our steps.

Making a plan is a good exercise. Because we only see in part, even our best plans are only partial. Something is always missing. The larger image in our minds must be the picture of God's love that is always directing us forward and deeper into his heart.

Maybe you need to get a different perspective and see how God views your plan. We are like a child with a box of crayons trying to color within the lines. Our plans are simply our best attempt to reproduce God's heart and desires as we see them.

We can plan each step in life, but it will be the hand of God that captures our feet and places them in the desired foothold. This is where your trust needs to be placed: in the directing love of God who will get you where you need to be.

Prayer

Father, I have a plan, but I only see in part. I hope the majority of this plan is what you want. I have tried my best. I know I didn't get this all right. Today, I rely on your faithfulness to put my feet where they need to be so I can walk forward in this process, deeper into your perfect will.

49

A Declaration

When you don't know the next step, declare the heart of God into the unknown. Declarations of God's heart will make a way when no way forward is visible.

Declarations uttered in faith are like spiritual bulldozers; they have the power to push aside walls of unbelief. These declarations call into being those things not yet visible to the natural eye.

God has made a way for you. Let your words express the joy that awaits you. Sing songs of deliverance before you are delivered. Worship before you have a reason to worship. Trust before your circumstances tell you trust is possible.

You are traveling on a new and unexplored course. You will not arrive at your final destination through human power or intellect. Your arrival at God's preferred future will come because at some point you stood where no trail was visible and called forth a pathway by declaring the heart of God.

Prayer

Father, I declare that you are good, and you have only goodness planned for me. I declare that your amazing love for me is both in this present moment and in my future. I declare an open way before me. You are my pathway.

50
Letting Go

Letting go will be harder than you think. Start letting go today, no matter how far in the future your transition may be.

In our grasping at life, we are trying to find a sense of security. Our grasping says: "As long as I can hold onto this present situation or relationship, I will be secure." This kind of security is an illusion. Nothing in this life is secure. The only secure things are what we place in the hands of God.

Letting go is not just a physical act—it is an emotional and spiritual one. This release must begin long before the date of your transition is a reality. Walk through all the phases of your coming transition with an open hand, grasping at nothing.

In our first major life transition, my wife, Jan, and I made plans to sell our dream home. Jan loved our home. During this time of transition, she would walk by the special kitchen sink and custom fireplace and release these items. She did this with our personal possessions and with our close friends we would soon leave. She did this for two years. In the end, when it came time to sell our home, Jan was free to move forward and not look back in regret. She never felt a sense of loss.

Try to disassemble this transition into its various parts and let go of one part at a time until there is nothing left for you to grasp. You want to approach the day of your transition empty-handed.

What part of your plan can you begin to let go of today?

Prayer

Jesus, I want to cling to my present reality as long as I can. I am not sure what I fear, but this death grip is an indicator that something is not right. I confess my fear of letting go. I invite your peace to come and show me what part of this process you want me to release before someone needs to come and pry open my clenched fist. Help me walk forward open-handed.

51

Perfection

Be realistic: you can always do a transition better. No transition will ever be perfect. "Perfect" is not the goal.

We have an unrealistic tendency to want our life transitions to be perfect. We need to revisit our definition of reality. In retrospect, each one of my transitions could have been done better, but people were involved. The human element changes everything.

If a "perfect" response to the plan is your goal, you will actually miss the heart of God in the plan. Whenever God relates to human beings, he builds into his plan recourse for human error. He understands your weaknesses. God can actually do more through your weakness than through your strength. His love doesn't operate through our inflated ego. God has chosen to work through the place of human weakness where the only thing we can bring to him is our humility.

"Perfect" is a strict, non-human attribute. Only God is perfect. If we require perfection as the goal of our transition, we will lose friends in the process because people will be people and end up failing us at some point. Because perfection is the person of God, not a goal, we can call upon him, the perfect one, to help us when we stumble.

Prayer

Lord, I lay down my demands and expectations for human perfection in this transition. It is certainly a sign of my imperfection and immaturity when I make these demands on myself and others. I renounce the judgments I have made without taking into account human frailty. You alone are perfect and good.

52

A Heart Condition

If you are serving the transition of someone who is your employer or supervisor, your main task is to watch the condition of your heart.

In a healthy, honor-filled work environment, the person transitioning may be blessed by financial gifts, severance packages, and trips to nice locales. These can all be part of a working relationship that honors long-term faithful service.

Early on, choose to celebrate each blessing the outgoing person receives. Celebrate the honor they receive like you were the one receiving the gifts. Don't miss the joy of blessing another person. Give honor where honor is due, even to someone who may have been hard to work with. You will never fail by giving honor.

Prayer

Lord, help me celebrate the life of [fill in a name]. Let my contribution, in word and deed, be large in substance and loud with joy. I bless and release them. I speak your love and favor over them as they take this next step in their life. I want their going to be covered in my blessing.

53
Feeling Used

At some point, you might feel used or even manipulated as you help someone else make a transition.

Planned transitions can take on a life of their own. Once plans get rolling, they can feel like a freight train running ahead at full steam. You either get on board or get out of the way. The process can feel pushy to those called to serve its ultimate goal.

We are called to serve one another. The only healthy way you can navigate this season is to put to death your ability to be offended. Offense is something you choose to pick up. Don't do it. People will see your negative attitude and how you hold yourself back when you should be pressing in.

You can never be manipulated if you have a servant's heart. Servants anticipate the needs of those they serve. They are too busy serving in love to be sidetracked by self-interest. Press in and God will do a wonderful work in your heart, and you will be a blessing to others.

Prayer

Jesus, I want to have a servant's heart. I don't want to serve with reluctance. Help me see the needs of others and show me how to serve those needs. Use me, Lord, in any way you desire. You came to serve and not be served, and that is how I want to live my life.

54

Valuable Lessons

We can learn some of our most valuable lessons from leaders who show us what we do not want to become. Not all wisdom comes from positive examples.

We can think the most valuable lessons are learned from the most honorable leaders. These faithful leaders do have much to teach us. There are, however, lessons to learn from those who have failed. From their failure, we can learn what *not* to do. Failure can be a powerful teacher if we allow God to have access to those places in our hearts where the failure was birthed.

The life of a leader in transition might anger you. Maybe what you see is wrong morally or ethically. Or maybe it is just a personal preference. You feel that if you were the leader, you would have done things differently.

In the meantime, what are your options? You can be offended and retreat into a place of judgment, or you can be offended and ask God to show you where in your own heart the same sin is possible or even in operation. In that invitation, you will begin to discover humility. Mercy will begin to flow toward those you had previously judged. Mercy and humility help us deal with our lack of love, and they act as a safeguard to protect us from going down the same road.

Prayer

Lord, it is easy for me to see sin in other people. As you reveal things to me, please reveal the condition of my own heart. Teach me about the same issues found in me. It is too easy for me to make other people the enemy and distance myself with a self-righteous attitude. Instead, I bless them with revelation, breakthrough, and turnaround.

55

Mystery and Wonder

In your transition, leave room for mystery and wonder. This is a spiritual endeavor, not a business plan.

Religion is mankind's attempt to codify God and have him all figured out. Man-made religion is devoid of the mystery and wonder that exists when we relate to the eternal God. He is so large that we will need all of eternity to explore his depths.

Whenever we lack a sense of mystery and wonder, we find ourselves attempting to control every aspect of the process and its outcome. Human control drains wonder and mystery from the process.

God wants to amaze you. God wants you to worship in wonder and awe when other people think you should live in fear. Your journey is a spiritual journey. See it from that perspective, and you will live in a sense of awe at what God will do in and through your life.

Prayer

Lord, I want to be like a little child who sees the brightly wrapped presents under the tree on Christmas morning. I want to run into the living room like I did when I was six years old and have my breath taken away at what I see before me. Birth in me wonder and mystery as I walk forward toward this new destination.

56

The Deposit

Your life has made a deposit and left an impact. In this life, you will not be able to fully define your influence. Eternity will reveal the significance of what you left behind.

Every human being makes a deposit in life, both good and bad—and sometimes ugly. Some of these deposits appear large, and some go unnoticed.

We all desire to exit our life with a banner over our heads that says, "Significance." We have been created to live a life of significance and leave behind an honorable legacy.

My understanding of legacy has changed dramatically over the years. There are still some lingering elements of self-focus that will surface from time to time—more often than I would like to admit. But I want my understanding of life and legacy to resemble what the Apostle Paul wrote to the church at Philippi: "For his sake I have discarded everything else, counting it all as garbage, so that I could gain Christ" (Philippians 3:8). Our legacy will be written from those things we were willing to discard for the sake of Christ.

Prayer

Lord, I want my memory to be an honorable one. I invite you to define the true value of my legacy by what I have chosen to discard for your sake, not what I have tried to hold on to for my own.

57

The Crowd

When the crowds came to Jesus, he did not try to hold them. He fed them and walked away. Compromise comes when we try to hold the crowd.

If you have experienced a certain degree of success, you may have attached some of your ego and identity to that success. This is a challenge because it makes it harder to let go of what is known, familiar, and affirming.

Jesus was always walking away from "success." He healed people and walked away. He fed the crowds and walked away. He did this because he knew his success was not to be enshrined and become a stationary monument. Even his disciples wanted to build memorials to his ministry.

In this transition, you will need to walk away from the crowds if you are to remain healthy spiritually.

Compromise rears its ugly head when the applause and evidence of your success tell you to create systems to hold onto the blessing. You may find yourself trying to recapture what happened in the past or building a memorial to your successes. Let the crowds follow Jesus. The only safe place for them to assemble is around him.

Prayer

Lord, I love to see people with spiritual hunger seeking your face. The crowd can be 10 or 10,000—it doesn't matter. I open my hands in order to not hold on to people. Deliver me from the evil that says this is about me and not about you. Reveal any hidden places of self-deception. I desire to be vulnerable and trusting as I walk in the light of your presence.

58

Crossing Frontiers

In your transition, you will cross a spiritual frontier. All spiritual frontiers have demons guarding them. Don't ignore this reality. Stepping through the gates of transition will cause them to react.

Every physical crossing recorded in scripture was a spiritual crossing. These crossings were guarded by dark spirits whose primary assignment was to detour and delay God's people through fear and discouragement.

This is not just a simple life adjustment you are making. You are crossing into destiny. In this crossing, you will come face to face with demonic powers whose primary assignment is to prevent you from crossing over into your destiny. They have been placed there purposefully to try to foil the plans of God.

You may have forgotten that your battle is not against flesh and blood. You may even think the problem is just you and your personal issues. The battle is larger; it is a spiritual battle in which you are contending against dark forces. This is your reality check.

Prayer

Father, open my eyes to see this spiritual battle. Let me see what I am contending with, so I can know how to battle. Lord Jesus, you have all authority and power over every dark spirit assigned to oppose and divert this plan. You have given that authority to me. I stand today in that authority and command these opposing spirits to step aside as I move forward into the future you have planned for me.

59

Available to God

In this transition, you will need to make yourself more available to God than to people.

Jesus loved people, but there were times when he needed to get away to process life alone with the Father. Some answers only come in times of separation. The deeper you get into this transition, the more you will need to make yourself available to God.

When Moses went to the mountaintop, he was enveloped in the cloud of God's presence. We are told the people heard him talking to God, and they were able to trust him because of that dialogue. People trust us more when they know we have been with God.

Look again at your schedule. Make room for time away with God so he can make those subtle adjustments with you when he has your undivided attention.

Prayer

Father, I admit that I find it too easy to give away my time with you to people and to my work schedule. Help me learn how to reserve time and space to develop a deeper intimacy with you. Help me create a place where you have my undivided attention.

60
Ending

Ending is far more challenging than beginning.

Ending is more challenging than beginning because over the years since we first began this journey, we have learned how to do so many things in our own strength. In the beginning, we leaned on God more because we did not yet possess the techniques and skills that can cause us to work without a dependency on God.

In the beginning, our faith was raw. We stepped out in faith into a vulnerable place. We were unknown and untested. That raw, faith-filled approach to life cannot be abandoned if we are going to finish well.

To end well requires that we rediscover a fresh and child-like faith. This kind of faith carries nothing in its hands that resembles self-sufficiency. This kind of faith is honest and admits that what is about to take place is as raw and new as our first steps of faith taken many years earlier.

As we walk forward, we hold the testimony of past seasons and a promise for our future. We have been practicing this life of trust over the years—entrusting ourselves to a faithful Father. With each step of faith, we go deeper into a place of mystery and wonder.

Prayer

Lord, it is too easy for me to assume that just because I have been walking this path for many years that I have what it takes to finish well. I come to this end looking for a new road: a road raw with possibilities. Help me see this as a beginning more than an ending. I place my trust in you, once again, until the very end.

"And I am certain that God, who began the good work within you, will continue his work until it is finally finished on the day when Christ Jesus returns."

—Philippians 1:6

Author Page

Ministry website:
www.garriselkins.com

Ministry address:
Garris Elkins
Prophetic Horizons
P.O. Box 509
Jacksonville, Oregon 97530
USA